My Sister Helped Me Heal

Vol. 2

The Power of Kingdom Sisterhood

Visionary: Chavon Anette

Dedication

A Generation of Women who have been Naomis to so many Ruths.

A Generation of Esther's rising to take their place!

Table of Contents

Foreword

Destiny Inspire

Pain, trauma, trials, fear, and defeat. The question is, how does one face it alone? How does one continue to go on while yet wearing a smile? The great Langston Hughs said it best, "We wear the mask."

Yet, in this hour, it takes sacred safe spaces of sisterhood to help heal the places we fear to reveal as women. It takes boldness to remove the mask of mistakes, mediocrity, and a world of make-believe and finally believe in the divinity that lies in each of us.

As a master certified life and confidence coach to women, I have witnessed the remarkable healing that has taken place in the hands of a HER! We have seen in scripture how Jesus showed much compassion to women who gently washed his feet with tears and dried them even with their hair. How much more does a woman help wipe the tears of a friend, sister, aunt, or mother.

Sisterhood is uniting women with the capacity to make real resilience. Women who realize they possess the spirit of a warrior. Women who identify as the feminine brought from the man's rib yet are fierce forces that the enemy fears. As a coach to women, I often remind Queens that they are not bound to choosing "either/or," but embodying both/and, and all of the above.

It is pieces of work such as this spearheaded by Chavon Thomas, a wise woman, warrior, and watchman that challenges us to see that we also can turn pain to power and tragedy into a triumph that speaks boldly of one's inner truth. I have watched her words come forth as hot coals from a fire and not a single word falling to the ground. I've seen the fierce fire of God proceed from her and pierce the pains of those assigned to her purpose. To know her is to be transformed by what she brings. A Queen who has courageously conquered and overcame.

The greatest book known to humanity said it like this, "They overcame him by the blood of the Lamb, and by the word of their testimony." Revelation 12:11

We all have a story, yet each woman has made the daring decision to reveal hers to help her sister heal. Reading this book is the beginning of an unbelievable breakthrough for you too.

Destiny Inspire
The Confidence Queen

Chapter 1

Fear, Loose Your Grip and Let Her Go
by Chante Smith

"Chante, you talk too much." "Stop talking." "Be quiet." "You do not have to say everything you feel." "You are just like your deadbeat daddy," were words that I constantly heard as a child growing up. As the oldest, I was always blamed for my sister's mistakes even though I did nothing wrong. "You're supposed to be the example." And as a child, who are you to 'talk back' or defend yourself when you know you had nothing to do with what they did. Every time I would try to speak, my mother shut me down.

In elementary school, I was even muzzled and shut out, teased that my voice was deep and that I sounded like a boy. I was treated like an outsider to the point I began to be afraid of even speaking my mind in peer groups. It became so normal that I just took it and would often hide in my room or closet just to get away. I would even hide in the bathtub so that they would leave me alone. So, I decided that the only person I would talk to was God.

As I grew older, I was walking in an identity placed on me, not by God, but by the one who was to nurture me and carry the weight that didn't belong to me. It was heavy. It was painful, hurtful, and low. I felt isolated, lonely, and alone. As I continued to grow up, the pain caused me to lash out in anger, bitterness, sadness, and eventually led me to be depressed and rebellious. I was now emotionally afraid to even speak my thoughts. At work, the fear of speaking would cripple me to anxiety where I would get nervous about speaking or giving a suggestion. I would have panic attacks and would just cry. I knew I had something to say, but I just couldn't get it out.

The fear of speaking and even who I really was, the one God created me to be, continued into my mid-late 30s. I was afraid of evening singing and leading songs. They hated the way my voice sounded over microphones and recordings. Every time I spoke and recorded it, I would not go back to listen because what I heard did not match what I was hearing in my head. Even when it came to making decisions, I felt like I wasn't confident enough to make it independently and still wanted my mother's approval or blessing. I was tired and ready for change. I was done with being locked inside this cave when I was only brought food at the cave entrance. That's when my process of transformation began.

I turned 41 in November of 2020, moved to another state on the east coast from Texas by way of engagement and made the first decision for the rest of my life on my own. The fear of what people would say and the warfare I received leading up to the move from my mother was hurtful, but I trusted God. See, God had instructed me to reach out to a young woman by the name of Chavon Annette. I connected with her months before I moved and stayed connected to her. As she ministered, God spoke through her the language for what I needed clarity. It was time for the transformation to happen. I was ready, and so was God.

I was so desperate for change and to stop being afraid to speak and even be me that I hired her as my mentor. I could feel pieces of the mold that covered me fall off like a statue crumbling piece by piece during that time. I was becoming, and I was loving the healed Chante. God would often use Chavon to speak words of encouragement like, "YOU ARE BEAUTIFUL" "YOU ARE CHOSEN" "YOUR VOICE IS NEEDED

AND NECESSARY." Those affirmative words I needed saved my life and restored me to God's original plan for me.

Chavon had just launched her coaching certification program, and I immediately signed up because I wanted to coach women into their purpose as well and reach back. During one of our classes, the spirit of God moved heavily through the zoom, and when it came to me, I knew something was about to break off. I was still dealing with self-confidence and fear of opening my mouth and speaking. Chavon got to me and led me into an entire deliverance of breaking off the fear that had gripped me for *soooooo* many years. I cried and decided to let it go. I felt it snap in half in the spirit, I knew I was no longer bound, and I was set free.

Chavon doesn't know that her being authentic and open showed me that it was ok for me to trust women again. That authenticity of really caring for God's people helped bridge the gap between my broken relationship with my mother and taught me how to just trust God again with female connections. Because of Chavon Anette, my mentor, friend, and sister, I have been able to speak boldly about what God has done, who God is to me, and just love the woman I am becoming. I've accepted the women God has also called me to partner with and be in friendship with.

Fear has officially been broken off my mouth, identity, womanhood, and call. I can boldly and sincerely say, My Sister, Chavon, Helped Me Heal.

Bio

Chante' Smith is a woman of God who has a passion for educating and training people on how to believe and see beyond their circumstances. Chante' is a Certified Life & Recovery Coach, Certified Christian Counselor Coach, and is known as the Activation Queen. She helps others overcome the life challenges that she herself had to walk through and overcome.

In addition, she is a self-published author, who has a few transformational projects that are set to release by the end of 2022. Her mission in life is to make an impact on the lives and opportunities that she is surrounded by.

Chante Smith took a huge leap of faith and moved from her home state of Texas to Virginia by the obedience of the Holy Spirit to begin her journey of taking care of her mental health

Chante' is a loving and supportive wife, the proud mother of 4 (two of which are her bonus children), a sister, a daughter and a loyal friend. She is a world changing, impact making, servant leader.

Chapter 2

Pots, Pans, and Prayers

By: Cee Cee Wrenn

The kitchen is where life lessons and teachings begin, from generational recipes and the meaning of a kitchen mechanic. At eight years old, I learned to cut my first onion in my mother's kitchen, which is a sous chef job in most restaurants "onion duty" with each cut of this onion, tears began to roll down my face. In my mind, I was thinking, *Why would my mother give me something to make me cry?* She looked up at me and said, "You are not done with this onion yet?" My reply was a loud, "NO." My eyes kept crying. She looked at me with her 1000 watt smile and said, "Welcome to my kitchen where life happens, but prayers will bring you through." On that day, I learned that an onion makes you cry because that's their defense mechanism to protect them from harm, so it releases a "sulfur gas" that causes our eyes to tear up. She said, "You will be alright. Finish cutting my onions and throw them in the pot when you are done, and remember, I am your mother. I will always protect you."

Believe that life is working for you, not against you. Things can go wrong in life. They inevitably do, and I learned a great lesson about trusting and being resourceful, even in the face of what looks like a disaster.

You are what you think. The most powerful thing you can do is to keep your thoughts and intentions positive, especially when you are whipping something good in the kitchen on a Sunday afternoon or any day. My mother always said some good music could set the tone in life and in the kitchen. She would sing as she stirred the pot or put the biscuits in the pan, she would sing all genres of music, but most of all, it would be the Gospel music that would bring so much emotion that she would be in her own praise and worship right in her kitchen. And that's why today, nothing sounds better in my kitchen on a Sunday afternoon like Gospel Music.

Life is, live it. Focus on what is working and what you have in the here and now. You thought you had garlic powder, but when it's time to add it, you realize you must have used it up last time. Or maybe you have all the ingredients, but you don't have enough of one thing or another. Instead of getting tripped up by what's not there, improvise, be open to whatever is and move forward with what you have.

Failure is trying to be perfect. Don't be afraid to be adventurous in life or in the kitchen. But don't hold yourself to outrageous standards.

When you don't know what to do, do nothing. If I'm out of options or running in circles trying to find a solution or make something happen, I've found that I'm trying too hard. I need to breathe. I need a moment to get still so I can hear what life wants me to do. When you feel the heat building and the countertop starting to spin, stop what you're doing and take a deep breath to get your bearings. Just be still and be in the moment, and you'll be surprised the knife you were looking for is right there in front of you.

Run toward what you fear. I've done this more times than I can count and might even be good at it. There's nothing more satisfying than doing something you've never done before and succeeding with a little practice.

Be "thankful" despite the situation. Be grateful and thankful, too, for those folks and experiences that were sometimes hard and brought heartache and pain. Sometimes it's hard to be gracious and kind to someone that has brought you pain; it's also powerful to be a blessing after the hurt.

Be kind to yourself. We are so hard on ourselves, even in life and in the kitchen. When our timing gets a little off, we end up with the guilt of not being perfect at the moment. Like my mom always stated, anything prepared with love tastes better than you think. Stop making apologies and let everyone enjoy you and your food, including yourself.

You got this. Take responsibility for your successes and your failures. You know what they say about too many cooks in the kitchen or too many people in your life can be chaotic. Everyone shouldn't have access to you or your kitchen.

Everyone has a way they like to do things. Everyone thinks their mac&cheese or their mama's mac&cheese is the best. But you've got to make your own way through life and your kitchen. Your recipe comes from using your own favorite ingredients, your own traditions, and what you've learned from your own experiences, good and bad. Always listen to your instincts. That doesn't mean someone else's mac&cheese is wrong. With an open mind, you may be able to pick up things here and there that you'd like to add to your own.

Life can be messy, takes a lot of practice, patience, and happens at warp speed. Even the peak moments are gone too soon, leaving behind a lot of work still to do, like that mountain of dishes that needs washing after an exquisite dinner party. Cooking, in fact, has been one of the greatest teachers in developing the woman I have become. It can be instantly rewarding, a grand celebration of flavor. Or it can turn quickly into a life lesson, keeping you humble with lots of opportunities to learn about the power of prayer, loss, imperfection, acceptance, perseverance, grief, willingness, and ultimately simple forgiveness that leaves you with a choice to either throw in the dish towel or try again.

Maintaining your perspective on things will help you overcome adversity even when you struggle, turning tough times into great experiences.

Bio

CeeCee Wrenn, by profession, is an Anesthesia Assistant for a major hospital corporation. By passion, the owner of AlwaysKissTheCookVA, which embodies custom spices and seasonings that will elevate your everyday cooking and taste buds on an unforgettable spice journey, catering services, cooking classes, and event hosting. A cookbook author of "OH TASTE&CEE", easy personal and generational recipes to elevate your cooking skills to the next level, currently working on the second cookbook. A 2021 ACHI MAGAZINE Editor's Choice Award recipient. AlwaysKissTheCookVA has been featured on TV, The Hampton Roads Show and WPCE radio. AlwaysKissTheCookVA hosts a dinner guest series called "Guess Who's Coming to Dinner", eating and talking over a home-cooked meal. It also did a live cooking segment for a 1million people platform, Girls Nite Live. Guest feature on Power and Grace Leaders Podcast and Talk Show, and God's Love Covers Podcast.

Follow and keep up with AlwaysKissTheCookVA on all social media platforms.

Chapter 3

God, But I Prayed!
By Amanda Smith

The alarm clock originally woke me up on March 8th, 2021. I snoozed it because I still had a little time before I needed to get up for my class. I got a call at 8:19 am. Barely awake, I looked and answered, "Hello." On the other end of the phone was a soft but panicky voice. "Amanda, what are you doing?" she asked. My response was, "I'm asleep. What's up?" She then said, "Noooooooo, Cede'Drion is dead!" From that moment, everything stopped for me. I threw my phone, and all I could do was scream in agony over and over again, "Noooooooooo, Lord nooooooo, why me?" But I prayed for him. I was so angry with God!

The night before I received that call from my son's stepmother, gunshots were reportedly heard in his neighborhood in Fayetteville. He lived there with his father for the last two years of high school. Police arrived where the reports came from, drove around, and saw no such evidence, so they left. They didn't know that my son had run three blocks from the scene, trying to get home but collapsing in his neighbor's yard. The collapse was caught on a ring camera from another neighbor's house. My son was found the next day by his dad when he was taking his daughter to school.

To hear that he had been out there all night, twelve hours to be exact, by himself was so heartbreaking, and it literally crushed me. I blamed everyone, even myself. Even though I did not find him, the visions were still in my head, and I could see everything as if I was there. I dreaded having to tell my other children, his younger siblings, the news. I was not prepared, but I knew I had to do it. Once I told them, all I wanted to do was hold them and tell them things would be ok, but I felt that was a lie deep inside. I felt empty. My husband tried his best to console me, but nothing seemed to work. I just wanted my son back. My phone kept constantly ringing, and my home filled with so many family members that I had not seen in a while trying to comfort me. But it just didn't work. I felt no one knew my pain, so no one could help me.

I was filled with so much anger, guilt, sadness, and depression that took over me. I had many thoughts of leaving this world because the pain was unbearable. I didn't want to even close my eyes because all I could see was him. I began to feel like I needed to rely on medications, but they did absolutely nothing for me, which intensified my thoughts of leaving. I knew I had to be there for my kids. I didn't want them to grow up without a mom like I did. But was that enough to keep me? It was just me, my husband, and the kids. Shortly after, all the calls, texts and visits stopped completely, and I felt alone. My husband and I agreed to seek therapy for the whole family. We went to therapy, but it didn't last long. The therapist talked about her family drama, diagnosed me with PTSD, and referred me to a prescribing doctor for medication. The final straw was when she offered my husband to use his sessions to take a nap instead of getting help.

I remembered receiving a text from an old acquaintance, Christina Russell, but I call her Silina, whom I had lost contact with before. She was sending her condolences and letting me know if I ever needed support that she could help me. Later, Silina texted me again to follow up, which was right on time. She let me know I could call her at any time, no matter what. For her, that wasn't just a cliché statement; she really meant it. I got more out of our forty-minute conversations over the phone than I did with the therapist. Speaking to her helped me in so many ways. She got me to see that I needed to begin to forgive in order to start healing. Even though she never experienced what I had experienced, her own trauma she used helped me to see better. She supplied me with a technique that I still use. Which is to keep praying for those who I blame and keep saying to myself, "I forgive them," until I really feel it. She reassured me that it was ok to have my moments and feelings, just don't stay there. She has helped me through this pain and through my marital issues at the same time. She encouraged me to write in a journal every day about my feelings which now is becoming a book to hopefully help others

Later in the year, I attended a networking event for women, and that's when I met Coach Dana Barnett-Watson. Afterward, I reached out to her for book/life coaching services. Dana has provided me with the direction and skills to heal from my past so that I can help heal others like myself. She helped me to realize after all the years of trauma I experienced in my life, it was not my fault. Once I realized it wasn't my fault, I began to really heal. Our sessions were always on point. She had the discernment to know when something was wrong and helped me get through it. She helped me to see my pain has a purpose. She helped me to ELEV8TE!

Grief can destroy so much without the proper support. Both ladies have been my rock in the most difficult times. They encouraged, motivated, and inspired me to be what they were for me to others. Most importantly, they prayed for me when I couldn't do it for myself. That's why they are my sisters who helped me heal.

Bio

Amanda Smith, wife of Leon Smith and mother to (in order of age) Cede'Drion, Miguel, Isaiah, Sarai, and bonus daughter Tatiyanna. She and Leon are co-owners of The Deluxe Affair, LLC. Amanda was in the medical field for eighteen years, starting as a PCA in 2004 and now a Licensed Practical nurse for nine years. While working as an LPN, she pursued her bachelor's in nursing until March 2021. Tragedy in March of 2021 hit her hard, and her calling changed. Although she has always wanted to be in the medical field, her caring heart, willingness, and desire to help never stopped, the way she wants to help just changed. She became the owner of I Haired That Boutique, LLC, where she is a Loctician and is also the Founder and President of CJW Changing Lives Foundation, which she started in honor of her son Cede'Drion. Here she provides community and youth services. Working with the youth in the past has equipped her to perform actively as a youth leader. She is now a co-author of My Sister Helped Me Heal vol 2. She is also the author of her upcoming books, Growing Pains: Breaking the Silence Series I, Growing Pains: Sunshine in My Mourning Series II, and A Mother's Journal: Grief Through Their Eyes. She is a certified healing coach and youth mentor who seeks to be a part of the community to help heal and not hinder. Amanda is an advocate for the youth and hopes to reach one child at a time. She hopes that her story reaches many who are lost to find their way back! Connect with Amanda via her website:

www.cjwchanginglivesfoundation.com or email
cjw.changinglivesfoundation@gmail.com

Chapter 4

A Tribute Speech

by Annie Nimely

This is a tribute to a woman whom I now know as a mentor, sister, and friend. Over the course of my life, a handful of individuals have impacted my life in major ways, but somehow, you have been there some of the most hectic… well, more like malicious, psychotic, oppressive, lost, and overwhelming times of my life. Times of my life that, let's say, I'd never want to go through again. How you've altered my life over time without even knowing it.

In high school, which now is a blur, I remember when you would engage with us after school during young life. You were one of the young life leaders for Green Run High. I didn't think it then, but your energy caught my eye. The way you laughed with us, danced with us, and were available to speak with us all stood out to me. I said to myself, "I like her; she's cool," but I wasn't ready to take my chances with you then. I thought high school would be the end of it. Little did I know you'd pop up years later.

Now I'm in college, and life has been a roller coaster. I've failed a couple of classes, taken some for the second time, and started working to pay for some expenses. One beautiful Sunday, I went to a service with a new friend and there you were.

You remembered me! You hugged me, and we took a picture to remember that day forever. You smiled, and I smiled back, but little did you know I wanted to end it all. I wanted to pack my bags, move to mars, and pretend earth never existed. After that day, we grew closer.

Chavon Anette Thomas, your confidence, prudence, and how you choose to unapologetically be you every day ignited a part of me that I did not know existed. How you've conquered the different adversities in your life and have stood by others during theirs altered my perspective of the world and people.

Chavon Anette Thomas taught me to be afraid and still walk through the fire. You taught me to take the leap of faith and know that I will not fall to the ground even when things don't work out as planned. You taught me that change is not a race but a fiery process that produces diamonds. You taught me that being strong doesn't necessarily mean carrying the world on your shoulders by yourself.

When I see you, I see some of the characteristics of the person I want to be when I grow up; bold, confident, determined, and sturdy. If I believed in coincidences, bumping into you was one heck of a coincidence.

Bio

Annie Nimely was born in Guiglo, Côte d'Ivoire. She came to the United States with her father for a chance at the American dream. Annie lives in Virginia where she serves as one of the worship leaders at All Nations Worship Assembly Virginia and executive board member of Power & Grace Leaders. She is a college of sciences graduate from Old Dominion University who majored in biology. Because of her love to serve and women's health, Annie aspires to become an OB/GYN. She hopes to travel the world and give back to those in need.

Surface Pressure

by Brienna Taylor

Looking back, 2021 was the hardest year of my life. I lost everything. In August, my spiritual father passed away, and on that same day, my son tested positive for covid. I couldn't be there physically for his wife like I wanted to, but God made a way. Whenever she needed to cry, vent, or even share her experiences, I was there on the receiving end. Our relationship grew into a sisterhood I had never experienced in my life. I became a part of her community when she needed it most. Who would've thought the same sister I helped grieve a great loss would be the same one I would call on just four months later?

On December 12th, 2021, at 5:08 pm, my mother was pronounced dead. Another parent gone just like that. I didn't even know what grieving would look like for me personally. Being in the church so long, I didn't even know it was possible. In the past, whenever I went through anything, old leaders told me to "suck it up," "get over it," "everyone is going through something," "push through," and in that moment, that's what I did. In that hospital room, I cried and held her hand until the warmth of her skin left. By then, more family started to come in, and I comforted them.

Just four short days later, my grandmother passed on December 16th. I was devasted. Instead of preparing for Christmas and shopping for gifts, I was writing my mother's obituary. My job only offered me three days each for my mother and grandmother's bereavement leave, but it wasn't enough, and I was forced to quit during it all. December 27th, I buried my grandmother, and the next day was my mother's funeral. December 30th, I drove back to Texas from Wisconsin with my children, some of my mother's keepsakes, and her ashes. That following Monday, I met with my boss. She informed me that by law, I could no longer live at the apartment if I was not an employee. One of the worst feelings in the world anyone could ever experience is losing a mother, grandmother, job, and housing in just a matter of weeks.

I became numb. I sat in that homeless shelter with guilt and shame trying to consume me. Mentally, I tormented myself so much about what people would say and think. I told no one I was there. I suffered in silence. One of the darkest moments of my life was in that shelter. My world was at a standstill, but I still had to perform day in and day out as if nothing had happened. I tried to make the best of it by playing card games, watching movies, and playing music with my kids, but it wasn't enough.

One night, a sister called and asked me, "Truly, how are you?" And I didn't hold back. Right then, she told me it was ok to have a human moment. She understood that so many people were pouring into the prophet, but no one was pouring into the daughter. I broke down immediately. She helped break down my walls and gave me the encouragement I needed to open my mouth and ask for help.

From there, I had the courage to call another sister. As I broke down to her, she told me, "Be selfish!" She told me it's ok to put myself first in this season and not rush the process! Out of habit, black women are forced to move on after a traumatizing experience as if nothing had ever happened since slavery, and now, 500 years later, it was happening to me.

This time, I dared to call my sister, who had experienced great loss, for help, and that's when it all shifted. She told me I was doing better than I thought. She explained how grief is not something to get over, but I must walk through it. I got a new job, a new house, and a new truck, and she showed me how to celebrate those milestones. The enemy tried to make me feel guilty for moving on with my life, and it was my sister who told me it was alright!

I never would've guessed how similar our journeys would be. She lost a husband, and I lost a mother, but our experiences were familiar. Right then, she became my community. Often, people assume that those grieving need space. We need support, and we have that with each other.

In that dark moment, she reminded me that I didn't lose my anointing. I was grieving with Grace and never stopped pouring! I never stopped sowing! I never stopped showing up! And I never stopped being a sister to her. What I gave out came back to me in an instant with sisterhood. What I sowed, I also reaped.

To the reader, if I can leave you with three things I've learned, they'll be this.

Number One: You're human, and God created you with emotions! Feel to heal! Don't block yourself or allow others to block you from that freedom! Crying does not make you weak; it makes you stronger! Do whatever you need to do to get it out, but you must feel it!

Number two: Be selfish! Take all the time you need for you! Only you and God can arbitrate your healing process! Only you and God can decide what that would even look like. You have every right to put yourself and your needs first!

Number three: Find community! Never allow the enemy to make you feel any shame, guilt, or even defeat when reaching out to people for help! I'll admit you can't go to everyone, so allow God to lead you to the right people. With the right help, you can heal properly! Most importantly, allow God to help you. Let Him be in your community! Don't count Him out.

Bio

Brienna Taylor is a proud native of Racine, WI but currently resides in Austin, TX, where she took her leap of faith. She is the mother of two beautiful girls and a son who has been diagnosed with Autism. Outside of her motherly activities, she's an Author, Transformational Coach, Breakthrough Mentor, Christian Counselor, Prophet, Psalmist, and most importantly, a Servant.

Her preferred name is Brie, and people call her "The Fire Starter." When she walks into the room, we know the atmosphere is about to catch fire and shift. Her business motto is "I am here to help you break out, break free, and break through!"

Breakthroughwithbrie.com

Chapter 6

The Testimony Heard Around the World

by Maude Freeman

I did not know anything about God when I met my future husband, Paul O. Freeman Sr. However, I grew up in Mt. Zion AME Church. I was married young, and we would be raising our first child from the beginning. My husband was not in church when we first met, even though his mom and three sisters were in the church at St. Stephens COGIC. Then, one night while we were married, I went to a revival, and a man was praying. I went up to the altar without being called, and the Lord touched me, and I ran. I remember wearing a green sweater suit that day and being pregnant with Gina Freeman. That day, I accepted Christ into my life.

After that moment, I went to church every Sunday at 6:00 am for prayer with Rosie Olds and other women at the church. However, although I had given my life to Christ, my husband was not saved yet. Nevertheless, I had faith that God could do it. I learned to pray with the women at St. Stephens COGIC. God brought me through, delivered me, and brought me out. The scripture God gave me to stand on was **Psalms 121:**

¹ I lift up my eyes to the mountains—
where does my help come from?
² My help comes from the Lord,
the Maker of heaven and earth.
³ He will not let your foot slip—
he who watches over you will not slumber;
⁴ indeed, he who watches over Israel
will neither slumber nor sleep.
⁵ The Lord watches over you—
the Lord is your shade at your right hand;
⁶ the sun will not harm you by day,
nor the moon by night.
⁷ The Lord will keep you from all harm—
he will watch over your life;
⁸ the Lord will watch over your coming and going
both now and forevermore.

These scriptures encouraged me for many days and still encourages me today. For example, I lost a sister who was nineteen years old. She became sick and experienced an aneurysm on the brain at the club and died that night. Margret Wilson came to my window that night and told me that my sister had died. I was hurt so bad because the Lord took my sister home, and I had just accepted Christ. My focus became that if I died, I would have to see God for myself, and I needed to be ready.

I continued to go to church and remain faithful to God. My family grew, and I even became a missionary in my church. Today, I am the president of the missionary board. However, I was still waiting for God to save my husband. I remember when I was talking to First Lady Walker now but Sister Walker back then, I told her, "I'm tired of my husband putting me out." She warmly replied, "Don't worry, it won't be long; a change is coming."

One day during a prayer meeting, I heard God say, "He is coming in, and it won't be long." After 24 years of waiting for God to save my husband, Paul Freeman Sr. got saved within the next 4-5 months. See, God had an appointed time. He accepted Christ into his life at forty-five years old. I knew I would never have to worry about him again.

Paul Sr. got saved, loved God, learned, and helped to clean the church. Later, Elder Burton made him a deacon, and they made him the president of the male chorus because my husband could sing. After he accepted Christ into his life, we served and praised God together. He died at age 57, but I am so thankful God saved him so that I could experience life with him by my side, serving God. The devil wanted me to go back to sin all those years I was saved and my husband wasn't. However, I was focused on serving God. Can you imagine if I had gone back for him? Where would I have been after he died, or what would I have done?

You must remember, like God told Jehoshaphat, the battle is not yours; it's God's. There is nothing God won't do. I experienced it for myself. I am thankful for all the women who were with me on my journey believing in God for my husband because it was not always an easy road. Today, I have three living sons and lost my daughter at fifty-four years old. Paul Freeman Jr. is a deacon in the church, and he has the same position that his father had over the male chorus and a Sunday school teacher. Kerry Freeman Sr. is an Elder in the church. Then, I am still believing God to save my son Walter Freeman because I know God is able. I have twelve grandchildren and twenty-one great-grandchildren. I am truly a blessed woman. In July this year, I will be celebrating my 80th birthday.

Bio

I am a lover of God. I am the president of the Missionary Board. I am a member of the Gospel Choir. I enjoy going to church, reading the bible, and praying. I started teaching the gospel almost fifty years ago. I did domestic work for over fifty years. Now, my focus is on God more so than ever. I will be eighty years old on my birthday, and my mind is on God to be an instrument of God. The most important thing in life is having Christ in your life.

Chapter 7

I Believe God

by Serleda Freeman

My husband and I received an alarming call from my mother-in-law the day after Thanksgiving. Maude Freeman was sharing with us that she was bleeding from her mouth, but she was sure that it would probably stop by the morning, and there was nothing to worry about. However, the next day we received a call from my niece that she was taking her to the hospital because she was still bleeding from her mouth. She was sent to the hospital, where they ran some tests on her. They said that she had an auto immune disease and she would need radiation. She was in the hospital for one week before she came home. After that, she came home to be with my husband and me to care for her until she got better. However, we had no idea this was just the beginning of the journey. They sent her home with us and told us to give her insulin, but there was no demonstration of how to do it correctly. We tried to get help, but her sugar dropped one day so low that my husband and I could not wake her up. So, we had to call 911.

When I went to the hospital, I looked through the curtains of her room, and she started having a seizure. The seizure terrified me, and I was screaming and crying so bad because they could not control her seizures.

They asked me to leave the room. I was truly scared to death. I called my husband, and he stated rushing to make his way to the hospital. Then, I called my brother-in-law, Kerri Freeman, in Maryland to give an update, and he immediately started praying. Due to the frequency of the seizures, they had to put her into a coma. It was truly a situation that was serious. She was placed in ICU, and there she was lying in bed with tubes everywhere and hooked to a machine that was keeping her alive. It was horrifying to see. When they went to take her out of the coma, she did not wake up right away. She was not talking and was unable to open her eyes. So, every day, I would bring prayer oil from the prayer team at my church, St. Stephens COGIC, where the pastor is Pastor Bruce Hughes, and the prayer team leader is Missionary Burton. I anointed her throat and said, "You will talk again," and I anointed her legs and said, "you will walk again."

This was a challenging time watching my mother-in-law go through this. My friends helped me through it: Mother Talley, Missionary Rhonda Gregory, Missionary Custis, Missionary Gaynell Burton, Missionary Caleta Rose, Missionary Beverly Cornick, Lisa Vann, Lady Ford, and Cynthia Macer. These women prayed, talked, and encouraged me through the process. On Wednesdays at 5:30 pm, I would come to her room and place the phone on speaker for her to hear the prayer call. One night, I saw her begin to move for the first time as Missionary Olds began to pray. When she finally began to talk again, I allowed her to talk with each one of my friends one by one to allow them to hear her voice.

After three weeks of being in the hospital, she finally returned to the house with my husband and me on Christmas day. There was a bed placed in a room near ours, and we took care of her. We were all so happy that she was out of the hospital. While she was with us for the next three months, my husband was amazing at taking care of his mom. He was sure to give her the insulin shots properly. He cooked her breakfast, lunch, and dinner. We worked together, taking care of her. When I had to work at night or a double, my nieces Monet and Maia would put my mother-in-law to bed at night, and when my husband and I went out to dinner, Monet sat with my mother-in-law.

In those three months, it was total care for my mother-in-law. As a Certified Nurse, I did my best to take care of her as I do at my job with patients. She had a physical therapist, and I continued lessons with her. The journey was not always easy. At one time, she started to become very irritable and aggressive. This was strange because I knew she was not under strong narcotics. She did not want to take her insulin, and she was acting in a way that she had not done. I talked with an LPN at my job about it, and George said it could be a Urinary Tract Infection. In older people, a UTI can have different effects. The Home Care Nurse came to the house to check her urine, and it was confirmed that she had what was suspected. When caring for older adults at home, I will encourage families to check on their family members when they start acting abnormally.

Then, there was a day when I noticed that she had not gotten up and come out of the room in a while. I walked into the room to check on her, and she was on the floor bleeding badly. We took her back to the hospital for the third time. They discovered blood clots, and because the blood thinner did not help, they inserted a stent. After this final procedure, she was able to go back to her own home. I still visited her to make sure she was taking her medication. I watched her get better and better over time. I took her to some of her doctor's appointments as she completed her radiation. Even when something serious happens, she still calls me.

This journey was not easy, but with the help of God, family, and friends, I was able to care for and support my mother-in-law. God worked a miracle before our eyes from ICU and now back at home doing well; God showed himself faithful.

Bio

Certified Nursing Assistant, Wife, Mother, Grandmother, and faithful servant of God. Been with my husband for 38 years and married 28 years. Member of St. Stephens COGIC. Member of the Elder's, Minister's, and Deacon's Wives Circle. Member of the Women's department.

Chapter 8

My Sisters Helped Heal Me
by Tiffany McDaniel

When I found out I was pregnant, I was a 26-year-old single minister. I had a one-night stand with a high school friend during low self-esteem, depressing season. I weighed the most I had at that point in my life; I had suffered yearly from seasonal depression during winter months since my teen years and did not know it at that point. But I had promised myself the year before that it would be my last year alone. I wanted to be married and have children and was rejected in love by who I thought would ultimately be "the one." I went through a season of random liaisons and still felt so empty.

I remember the night I got pregnant; it was a cold rainy night in January 1998. My phone rang, and I was asked out to dinner by an old friend, and I obliged. I remember feeling fat and bloated, my back and neck were hurting, which it often did when it rained, and I felt like an old lady. But the words and attention of my old friend made me feel alive again, even if for just a night. I tried to fight the feelings exuding from me that night, but I fought to no avail over the cascading waves of vulnerability that overtook my flesh.

That night, my son was conceived, I had no clue at the moment, but I felt so dirty and such a mess. I was a minister, intercessor, deliverance teamwork, altar worker, choir member and assistant director, and anything else I could find for my hands to do at my church as a young single woman in ministry. As my friend slept, I cried and repented for the act that we had just engaged in. As I sobbed in my bathroom, I felt the presence of God come over me, and I knew He was there with me despite how I was still feeling. I cried myself to sleep, and my friend left the next morning.

I had regular menstrual cycles at this point in my life, but that had not always been the case. I had a condition that caused severe bleeding, ovarian cysts, and horrible cramps, and irregular cycles. However, my last few cycles had run normally. So much so that when the next month came and I had no appearance of my period but did have soreness and a strange appetite, I took a test, and it was positive. I gasped and hit the floor. Again, in my bathroom, I went bawling my eyes out, and I heard God's voice so plain and clear.

"Get up, I am the Father, and I will take care of you all." I do not think I was ever so scared in my life. I knew that I had let God down. But here He was telling me from that moment that I found out that He would take care of US. So, I knew that I would make it alright in the back of my mind, but I almost immediately began to beat myself up psychologically. I told coworkers on my job, and they were happy and supportive. I told my best friend back home, and she originally thought I was calling to tell her that I had cancer due to having so many irregular pap smears and issues with my cervix. In fact, I was told that I would have difficulty conceiving, which ironically, I did not since the next time I had sex, I got pregnant.

When people at church found out, it was received with mixed reviews. Some were very disappointed, some avoided me, and very few came to love on and support me. They had no clue that I was not in sin. I had already repented for the act that created the pregnancy, but the careful care of my skin, hair, and outfits seemed to bother some who I guess would have preferred me be in sackcloth and ashes on the back pew. But God would always prompt me to continue praising and worshiping HIM, and I did, and it is what kept me alive, literally.

One morning, at the end of February, I woke up to blood running down my legs. I screamed, called my mom, and she told me to call my doctor. I did, and she instructed me what to do. After receiving an ultrasound that showed one fetus clinging to one side of my uterus, the other side was dark, denoting there might have been a fraternal twin on the other side that did not survive that was spontaneously aborting. I ended up being on and off bed rest from the end of February until the end of April. I relocated back to live with my parents in early May.

During my time on bed rest, it was a very grim time. In retrospect on my life's journey when I got pregnant, I was suffering from low self-esteem and depression, all while going to church several times a week, working every day. I was singing, smiling, and praying for others through their issues and feeling sad, rejected and hopeless within myself, too embarrassed to share how I really felt.

And then were my sisters who helped me heal….

My sister Yvonne gave me the first baby outfit that I hung in my closet. When I felt scared, I would take it in my hands, close my eyes, and sniff it. It was a yellow nightgown that said "hello" on it.

My nursemaid/sister Danielle would come over and stay the night at the drop of the hat when I called to tell her the bleeding had started again. She cooked according to my cravings even though they would come back up, and I felt so terrible after all the care she put into the meals.

My sister Joyce drove down from Ohio not only when I was on bed rest to tend to me and pray over me, but she also did the same to my baby shower in Virginia Beach when I moved back in with my parents. She put together a stroller/car seat combo by hand. My Sanders sisters kept me company, doing my hair, errands, and keeping me up on all things church and family.

My sister Kina threw me a baby shower before I left the DC area. It was quaint and touching that was attended by the singing group that we were in. And her mother was my sweet secret pal that year, constantly praying and giving thoughtful gifts and cards to bless me.

And then there was my youngest nursemaid, my baby sister Cece, who was in high school and would come on weekends to be with me. She was my little comedian, relieving my soul with laughter. She kept me in stitches and truly made my soul bubble with healing tears and cackles.

Finally, was my bester, Monica. I refer to her as my bester because I have known her as my best friend and sister for my whole life through every phase.

I was eight when I met her. When others bullied me, she took them on and protected me. When I went on bed rest up 95 North, she came to care for me as only she could.

When I moved back home, her care continued, and when I had to have an emergency c-section due to toxemia, which caused my pressure to shoot sky-high, triggering violent seizures, she was still there for me. Monica grabbed my mom and my Auntie Linda, and they prayed and recited Psalm 91 until we came through with my son! He was born ill, and I was ill for months afterward, but she cooked, visited, babysat, and drove for me. Her inspiration cards have peppered my life with perfect words at the perfect times to speak healing, peace, and encouragement like only she could. She often tags teamed with big sister Jessie who called, cried, prayed, travailed, held me down in the spirit and shielded many bullets from the enemy on my behalf.

My sisters helped heal me, and my son and I miraculously survived as proof.

Bio

Tiffany H. McDaniel, M.Ed. is a servant leader who is continually seeking to grow in the grace and the knowledge of the Lord Jesus Christ by empowering and encouraging others in whatever capacity God allows her to be in – preaching, teaching, singing, prophesying, interceding or whatever is needed for full body ministry to be activated. She is a veteran educator of over 20 years serving more recently at her alma mater where she was selected as Teacher of the Year at Green Run High School in Virginia Beach where she resides with her family. McDaniel was called to preaching ministry at the age of 20, prophetic ministry at 24 and currently serves as a licensed Prophetess under the leadership of Apostle Michael J. Rogers, Sr., Senior Pastor of Kingdom Cathedral and presider of the Bibleway Churches Worldwide. McDaniel looks forward to continuing to share her testimonies in days to come as God opens doors to do so.

Chapter 9

The Love of a Sister
by Dr. Monique Rodgers

As a little girl growing up, I remember how fun it was just to spend time with my older sister Abbigail. She, as the first born, carried a lot of responsibilities, one of which included watching me, who was her baby sister, while my mom went to work. She was also my protector when I went to school and was bullied by kids that were jealous of me. She made sure that they did not bother me. I remember one day in school when I received an enormous amount of bullying; I was crying and didn't want to go to school the next day. My mother dressed my sister and me up as twins. We always had matching outfits. Our hair was always done because my mother, as a cosmetologist and model at the time, did not tolerate anything less than the best for her daughters. My sister was extremely gifted in writing. As a straight-A student, she spent a lot of her time reading books while I spent mine creating art posters and writing books. It has been often stated that a sister's love can carry over even greater than that of our mothers, aunts, or grandmothers. There is something exceptional about the love of a sister. There is a unique bond that sisters share within each other that can often be alluded to as even a sister code. Sisters share experiences. They may fight and argue, but at the end of the day, they come back together because, as sisters, one rule remains - that love of a sister cannot ever be destroyed.

Once of my favorite movies that my sister and I loved watching together was The Sisterhood of the Traveling Pants and The Divine Secrets of the Ya Ya Sisterhood. In the first movie, a group of best friends has a special pair of jeans that they believe can bring a certain kind of help. Each friend later realizes in the end that their friendship and closeness together are greater than any pair of jeans. In the other movie, The Divine Secret of The Ya Ya Sisterhood, a group of close friends are connected and close and visit each other every day. In the movie, the mother and day have a small fight that causes them not to speak to one another, and it is the sisterhood circle that works together to get them to speaking and loving each other again.

Although I have never been in a sorority, I have had close knitted relationships with my dorm sisters from college at Oral Roberts University who have supported me, listened to me, and had my back. Throughout my life, it has been my sisters that have come in my life as extended family members that have blessed me and have helped me become better. Another special sister came into my life, and she helped me heal from my divorce. At the time in my life, I had to escape from a marriage that I knew was not the will of God for my life. She rescued me. That sister at the time helped me cope and heal from the pain and trauma that I had experienced over that year. She helped me rest, recover, heal, and regain my life again. I had to start over, but I am thankful to God for her. She allowed me to move in with her at the time and to get back on my feet. It took a year, but I spent time healing in that year. I am so thankful to God for her being there in my life for a time that I needed someone the most just to recover and heal. I am thankful to God that even though she was not my sister from birth, she helped me overcome one of the most broken times in my life.

Right now, I am praying for my big sister Abbigail currently in my life; we are not as close as we were as children. I pray every day that God will bring us closer and that I can spend time with her and share stories. The other sisters that God has now given me have also helped to bring healing to my life. God gave me new sisters that helped uplift me, build me up, and not compete with me or become jealous of me but simply love me and support me as a sister. The missing elements that we need in sister circles are support, edification, love, and prayer, which are the glue to sisterhood.

Bio

Dr. Monique Rodgers is an international best-selling author, CEO, Master business coach, Certified Vegan health coach, mentor, writing coach, ordained prophet, intercessor, visionary of Called to Intercede Volumes 1-8. Dr. Rodgers is also a literary genius and award-winning author. Some of her most recent accolades and accomplishments include being included in Kish magazine's Top 20 authors of 2021-2022. She was also included in Marquis Who's Who in America 2021-2022. She has been featured in magazines, podcasts, television shows, radio shows, and more. In 2021, Dr. Rodgers spoke at a Mental Health Symposium on the same stage as Carolyn Leaf and various others as in-person and virtual speakers. She has also been a host for her own tv show called, The Healing Zone in Atlanta. She is a former radio host for WDRB Media. Dr. Rodgers has also traveled to 6 countries on missions. She is also a global leader and ambassador. She serves as an ambassador for Kingdom Sniper Institute for Evangelist Latrice Ryan. She serves as a prayer hub leader for the city of Raleigh for Apostle Jennifer LeClaire. Her other servitudes include being on staff with Patricia Bailey Ministries as a social media manager.

Chapter 10

The Power of Kingdom Sisterhood

by Dr. Frances Bailey

What is power? Power is the ability or skill to do something. What is Kingdom? Kingdom is the authority of God and dominion. What is Sisterhood? Sisterhood is the relationship between women who are sisters. The Power of Kingdom sisterhood basically says that the circle of women who all serve the Lord Jesus Christ have God's ability and authority to encourage and push another sister into the dominion that God has promised us. There are plenty of sisterhoods, but not all Kingdom sisterhoods are operating under the authority of God. Nothing can match the power of kingdom sisterhood. I remember going through several trying times in my life, and if it wasn't for my sisters in Christ, I don't know if I could've made it.

Kingdom sisterhood has a balance by God being the foundation in which all things are possible. When going through this thing called life, it is essential to be surrounded by Kingdom sisterhood. Kingdom sisterhood talks differently than the world sisterhood. Their foundation and words of wisdom come from God's heart and mind. I am one to tell you how Kingdom Sisterhood helped me through many barriers and opportunities in my life. I remember going through a time of transition.

39

I felt so lost during this time. I remember asking God why I have to transition. Why do I have to be uncomfortable in this season? God started to show me that there were places in my life that needed to be healed.

Going through the process of greater inner healing was uncomfortable. God was removing the Egypt that was in my life, and it seemed like I couldn't see the positive because I was in the wilderness. I couldn't understand my process at the time and was just in a place of confusion. My emotions seemed to be running everywhere, and deep down, I felt like I was all alone. Sometimes, while on the journey that God has for us, it can become lonely and we can feel like we are all in this by ourselves, but God had to remind us of Kingdom Sisterhood. We don't have to fight alone. Your kingdom sister will fight with you. After all, the bible says that one shall chase a thousand and two shall chase then thousand to flight. In that instance, I tapped into the power of Kingdom sisterhood and called my sister to help fight with me during my healing period. I was so hurt in my emotions from the things I had gone through. I vented to my sister and cried tear after tear. She would listen and pray for and with me. There were times when I couldn't muster up the strength to pray for myself, but she would help cover me. There were times when I couldn't encourage myself, but she encouraged me. There were even times my flesh would try to direct me in the way of the world, but my Kingdom sister would hold me accountable in the word of God, letting me know the better way.

Kingdom Sisterhood doesn't encourage messiness or clap backs. Your kingdom sister doesn't have the world's viewpoints, nor do they conform to the world, so their wisdom and guidance keep you in the will of God. The power of Kingdom sisterhood picks up where you begin to fall short. It is the true definition of a sister's keeper. Your Kingdom sister doesn't join the pity party with you. She cancels it and then invites you to the victory party. I remember my Kingdom sister also being real about what she saw that I couldn't see. Your Kingdom sister will see you through the eyes of God and will tell you how to be more in the image of God in love. You don't always need people around to tell you what you want to hear, but you want them to tell you the truth. Kingdom sisters care more about your standing in the eyes of God than pleasing your ears. Even though they saw things that may need to be adjusted, a kingdom sister will love you through your flaws. You realize this and understand this as well if you are a kingdom sister to your sister.

Kingdom sisterhood isn't jealousy, envy, or backbiting. Kingdom sisterhood acknowledges and knows that we serve the same God that is no respecter of person; therefore, we win together. Kingdom sisterhood realizes that we are better together because we are many members in the body of Christ. We are all needed and essential. The power of Kingdom sisterhood is a beacon of light for those who don't really know what the real bond of love is. The power of Kingdom sisterhood demonstrates the true outlook of unity in God.

The power of Kingdom sisterhood has played such a huge role in my life. The unity and love shown to me during my happy and not-happy moments have been untouched. If it wasn't for my Kingdom sisterhood ensuring I stay in the will of God, I probably wouldn't be as strong as I am today. I love this sisterhood because I don't have to take a vow or pledge my life to be a sister to another, but because of who God is and he being our father makes us sisters. Kingdom sisterhood has helped me heal, love greater, become whole, and cherish relationships. When another is willing to suffer with you and bear your burdens, that's Kingdom. When another is willing to build you up when they aren't too strong themselves, that's Kingdom. When you have a person who loves you beyond your flaws and love you as they love themselves, that's Kingdom. I am forever grateful for my Kingdom Sisterhood. God knew I needed a Kingdom sisterhood during my transition to the next level, and I thank God for my sisters locally and globally. Kingdom Sisterhood is true sisterhood.

Bio

Born and raised on Eastern Shore of Virginia, Dr. Frances Ann Bailey is a God lover, International Amazon Best Selling Author, Podcast Host, International TEDx Speaker, wife, mother, philanthropist, and an Award-Winning Certified Coach and Certified Christian Counselor. Also known as the "Purpose Zeal Coach" is the CEO of Frances Bailey Enterprises, LLC, and the Founder/President of the nonprofit organization Red Door Empowerment. Frances has her Bachelor of Science in Criminal Justice, a Master's in Public Administration, a Doctorate in Leadership and a PhD in Business Administration and Entrepreneurship. Frances seeks to help women who were once like herself to overcome life's obstacles, break free from bondage, and recover from life setbacks to keep their zeal for purpose. Frances' expertise, testimonies, and wisdom has taken her before great individuals. To name a few, she been featured the Walden University magazine and Sheen Magazine

The Moment of Breakthrough

Everyone has a moment of breakthrough, but our stories reveal that it is not something that is done alone. God will send people to help you cross one of the largest hurdles in your life. Life is not supposed to be lived or even fought alone. God has made us relational beings in need of community like a sisterhood to help us navigate the areas of our lives that still need hope. Today, don't run from your calling or your purpose. Today, don't hide your pain from your friends. Make a choice to be vulnerable so that you can reach your place of healing. Then, return the love and be that for someone else. There is a common phrase, "Each one teaches one." Well, I say, "Each one heals one."

As God brings healing in your life through sisterhood, be an agent of change for someone else. You don't do the healing, but if you manage the moment with another sister with love, you can position them as a kingdom sister to reach the God who can heal them. Be an extension of the hand and heart of God as a sister. Job was asked to pray for his friend who misjudged him, and the blessings of the Lord for all that he suffered were released. Who are you praying for in this season? What sister needs your help? If Job was blessed for praying for those who mistreated him, God will bless you for praying for those who need a helping hand to navigate a dark season.

Don't underestimate the power of your prayer, time, love, or words of encouragement and affirmation. There is a sister waiting for their moment of breakthrough, and it could be you.

Let's make it our mission to help another sister HEAL!

About the Visionary

First and foremost, Chavon Anette is a daughter of God! Chavon is an Amazon #1 International Bestselling Author, Global Speaker, Leadership and Life Coach, and Talk Show Host. She is the CEO of Purpose Unwrapped, LLC and non-profit Power and Grace Leaders, Inc.

Chavon is affectionally known as the Fire Leadership Coach. She marries practical and spiritual tools to empower and equip kingdom people to lead in the world. She balances entrepreneurship, ministry, and employment as the Student Success Manager at Regent University. Her mission is to help Kingdom people Break Fear, Build Faith, and Lead Confidently online and beyond. She enjoys creating experiences for transformation, so she hosts annual two big events: Fanning the Flame Experience and Powerhouse Leaders Conference.

She is also a transformational speaker and minister of the gospel who speaks with great passion in a way that empowers and challenges her listeners. She has been featured as a speaker on ABC news, TCT Today, Virginia Wesleyan University, and at conferences and other events such as globally recognized Comeback Champion Summit, Sister Leads Conference, and more.

Chavon has published 4 books that are available on Amazon, and she has been a part of 7 anthologies. From Pain to Purpose was her first solo project that became an Amazon #1 Bestselling book. Three anthologies became Amazon #1 Bestsellers- Undeterred, (International Bestselling) Unveiled Transparency, Called to Intercede and Sister Leaders. She is the visionary of volumes of My Sister Helped Me Heal Anthology, which is an Amazon #1 Bestselling Anthology movement.

Chavon Anette was the 2021 Servant Leader of the Year Award Recipient from ACHI Magazine.